The Journey of an African Child

The Inspirational Story of My Life

STANLEY NGWA

FriesenPress

Suite 300 - 990 Fort St
Victoria, BC, Canada, V8V 3K2
www.friesenpress.com

Copyright © 2016 by Stanley Ngwa
First Edition — 2016

All rights reserved.

No part of this publication may be reproduced in any form, or
by any means, electronic or mechanical, including photocopying,
recording, or any information browsing, storage, or retrieval
system, without permission in writing from FriesenPress.

ISBN
978-1-4602-8370-7 (Paperback)
978-1-4602-8371-4 (eBook)

1. Religion, Christian Life, Personal Growth

Distributed to the trade by The Ingram Book Company

ACKNOWLEDGEMENTS

This book is dedicated to my entire family, my friends, and most especially to the following:

Abednego Ngwa Njifor, my late father, who worked so hard day and night to provide me with a future. Despite all the odds, he was committed to providing sound education to all of his children. My dad's level of education was equivalent to grade three, but that did not stop him from educating his children to university level.

Anna Bihlem Ngwa, my mother, who worked so hard to assist me even during very tough times when my dad was critically ill and even after his death. She became the breadwinner for the entire family.

Beatrice Ngum Njifor, my elder sister, whose salary was about $15 per month, but she saved every cent to assist me to continue my education. As I had no money to afford food, she provided most of the food I ate as a student. Thank you for your generosity.

Bridget Sirri Nsieh, my wife, who worked hard to support me in school, took great care of the children while I was in school, and continues to show us love as a wife and mother.

Thimothy Menkem Jong, a famous friend who was so instrumental in my life during my university education. Thimothy provided me with shelter when I needed it most.

Irene and Ephraim who changed my life significantly from a banana worker to a master of science student in Belgium. Your contributions are immeasurable and no amount of thank yous will ever be enough. What would I have done without you?

Greenfield a God-chosen friend who took care of me and provided me with shelter and finances during my studies in Belgium.

Walters, a friend who contributed part of my flight fare to Belgium, picked my family up from the Edmonton International Airport and hosted us for nine days. Your kindness is appreciated.

Godlove, a friend who picked me up from the airport in Brussels, Belgium, and provided me with shelter for two months. Godlove also assisted Walters in picking us from the Edmonton International Airport when we arrived from Cameroon.

David and Kathy, who helped us with beds, mattresses, and other household furniture. I do not know what we would have done without David and Kathy.

Dayspring Presbyterian church for moral, spiritual, and material support. Sheila who cashed my cheque in a bank where I had no account and Lucas who offered a gift of $ 200.00

Joanne and Ed for immeasurable assistance. May God replenish your resources.

Avy for accepting and distributing my resume to friends and colleagues.

Taras for hiring me and giving me a chance to proof myself.

Heather Tansem for editing and providing more clarity and meaning to this book. Your time and effort helped me realized my dream. Heather did all this at no cost.

Marilyn and Gordon for editing spelling and grammar at no cost.

The Canadian and Alberta governments for funding my oil and gas education (skills upgrade program) for one year.

All other men and women, boys, and girls who have played a role in my life and the lives of my family members.

Last, but most importantly, to all governments, corporations, and people around the world who have given a chance to underprivileged people to prove themselves. There is nothing more important than having the dignity to work and provide for the family.

INTRODUCTION

Life is a journey, which may be on a smooth or rough path. It may be long for some people and very short for others. Numerous factors may influence the outcome of this journey. Some factors may be within the circle of human influence while others may be beyond. Factors within human control can be assessed and adjusted. Have you had an opportunity to re-assess the journey of your life? How did you feel? Would you prefer to be on a different path? Would you try another approach to certain aspects of life if given a second chance? Have you taken responsibility for things that were not done right? Do you think your life story can play a role in someone's lives? Have you considered sharing your life story to make a difference in someone's life?

The purpose of this book is to share my life story and the adversities I have had to overcome. Personal stories such as mine may be educational to both children and adults who seek to understand how life operates in other societies around the world. It may be an opportunity for some people to compare and learn from my life experience. Forty-five years ago who would have predicted a poor boy born to two peasant farmers in a remote African village to be where I'm today? Certainly no one could have guessed. It has been a huge surprise to many people who knew me as a child and have seen me grow. Well, it has also been a surprise to me, especially when I reflect on where I was, who I was, and my family circumstances. I grew up with little to no hope of surviving hardship, malnutrition, and disease. I barely survived bites from poisonous snakes and scorpions. Human urine was used to treat snake poison. Can you drink your urine? What about someone else's urine? Do you think urine can neutralize snake poison? It was a myth in my days and still continues to be a myth in my village and other parts of the world today. It was a scary situation. When I think about it now it seem like a dream.

As I reflect on my past life circumstances I think of the many different strategies that have helped me survive as I strived to attain my goals. I could have given up, as my life was truly full of challenges and unbearable living conditions. Because of my immediate family, my extended family, some friends along the way, God's guidance, and my burning desire to be successful, I was able to overcome many adversities.

Before I begin my life story, let me first of all provide you with an outline of the rest of the book. Chapter One through Chapter Seven provides details of my inspirational life story, information about my immediate family, and our life circumstances in Canada. Chapter Eight describes a variety of life circumstances that people may find themselves in as well as many strategies I used to cope in similar circumstances. Chapter Nine is about the difficulties of underprivileged people around the world. Chapter Ten is about my beloved parents and in Chapter Eleven I talk about Canada, the land of opportunities.

My book is intended for any interested readers, but especially if you find yourself in a difficult or challenging circumstance. If that is so, it is my wish to help you with strategies and to give you hope.

CHAPTER ONE

The Story of My Life

For me to provide a complete summary of my life story I'll begin with a recollection of my childhood circumstances. In my days as a child, there were no cameras to take pictures during daily activities. I knew of one photographer who had a pinhole camera but he would only take pictures during important occasions or ceremonies such as marriage and annual dance festivals. The pictures were very expensive and many people, including my family, could not afford them. This explains why I lack childhood pictures to refer to for a better illustration of my story. Instead, I will have to go by memory.

My Childhood Circumstances

I am one of two boys in a large family of ten. I was born in the small village of Buwe-Bukari in Bafut, located in the northwest province of Cameroon, Africa. Infant and maternal mortality rate was very high in my village and across Cameroon at the time I was born. Unfortunately, this particular situation is only slightly better today.

At that time, the late 1960s, there were no nearby hospitals and only a few trained nurses in our village. Most doctors and nurses were residents of the cities. In my village, there were numerous tropical diseases and malnutrition, no subsidies of any kind, no health care coverage or benefits, no safety net for the poor, and no rights for the underprivileged. There was no potable water or electricity, no toys for kids, no milk, no yogurt, no comfortable beds to sleep on, but only bamboo beds with or without itchy grass mattresses. There were no paved roads and schools were located five miles away. Children did not have shoes to wear on sand and gravel footpaths. In school there weren't benches to sit on and there were no trained teachers; sometimes there wasn't even chalk for the untrained teachers and volunteers to write on the black board. You might have one exercise book for all subjects and for the entire academic year. Pit toilets were full of maggots and flies and located four to five meters behind each house. There wasn't any separate waste disposal system. Most of the time, the same running streams and rivers were used not only for bathing and as a source of drinking water, but also used for waste disposal. Farm work was the only source of income and it was excessively hard labor and barely sufferable.

My village has not changed much in the last fifty to sixty years. There are still children growing up and living in similar or even worse circumstances. And understand that my village is not an exception. There are many societies like these that still exist in the world today, but, sadly, there isn't anyone to tell their story. One logical reason that stories are not shared is probably due to the lack of access to communication technology in societies like these. In addition, some governments may be very oppressive in censuring information that gets to the rest of the world. Another factor is that the developed world may not pay attention to countries and villages where there is no economic or political interest. In such societies people are tortured and there is no one to defend or speak for them. In my village and other parts across Africa and the world there are many people working extremely hard 24/7 but they are still not able to live above the poverty line. In some societies no one really cares about such unprivileged people.

As a child between the age of one and four my mother carried me on her back wherever she went. She spent most of her time on the farm and working with her locally designed hoe. This was done all year round, even in the dry season when temperatures are in the mid forties degrees Celsius. In the rainy season there was torrential rainfall, sometimes with hailstones and thunder and we had no place to hide. Most of the time she would take a twenty-minute break once or twice a day to drink water and to breastfeed me. She did this for all eight children.

In my time, children six years and older were responsible for a host of daily activities including fetching water, gathering firewood, washing dishes, feeding all domestic animals (pigs, goats, fowls etc.), transporting food items from farm to home and from home to the market (located eight miles from home), go to school when possible, assist parents in the farm most of the time, and babysit younger siblings. In my village, the illiteracy rate was and is still very high. I believe this situation is the same or even worse in some African societies and other parts of the world.

My Responsibilities Between the Age of Six and Eight

Beginning at the age of six, my mother woke me up each day at five o'clock in the morning to start my daily routine. My older siblings, together with my father, had already left by three o'clock to transport food from the family farm. The first thing for me was to fetch water from the stream and from the spring, if it was flowing. Sometimes, especially in the dry season, the spring dried up. The only alternative left was to drink from streams and rivers. When both spring water and the streams were available, the spring water was for drinking and the stream water for dish washing and bathing. After fetching water, I washed the dishes and fed the animals. While I did these jobs my mother would be cooking food as my dad and older siblings would be due back shortly.

Our family farm was about fifteen miles away from our home. There were no roads and certainly no vehicles so everything had to be done by foot. Food items were transported by carrying them on our heads and my dad would determine the weight based on each person's age. The least weight for the youngest person would be about twenty kilograms and the older ones carried fifty kilograms or more. Whatever the load, it was usually too heavy for each person as no one was able to tilt their head or turn their neck left or right for quite awhile after dropping the load at home.

My morning duties were usually completed at about the same time that my older siblings returned from the farm. We took a shower together with the water I had fetched. After the shower, we ate and went to school. Sometimes when we left for school we had to carry food items on our heads that now needed to be transported to the market. It was convenient because the school was situated mid-way between our home and the weekly market. As we left for school our parents would either leave for the market or when it wasn't a market day, they left for the farm where they would spend the entire day doing manual labor. Since our parents worked all day, most of the time the older siblings took turns in taking our younger siblings, aged two to five years, to babysit while at school.

So going to school and getting schoolwork done was complicated. It wasn't like most young people, where they just get up and go to school to learn. We sometimes had to babysit, so it was hard to focus on what was being taught. We were also tired from our morning duties and ninety percent of the time we went to school late because of them. Each time we arrived late we received corporal punishment from our teachers. At times we sustained injuries, which nobody cared about. We worked so many hours at home or on the farm after school that there wasn't much time to do school assignments. It was extremely difficult to do well at school with all of these extenuating circumstances.

After school we went home and the afternoon assignment for kids of my age was to fetch water and gather firewood in the forest. The older siblings had to go to the farm and meet our parents. The firewood was for the evening and next morning's meal preparations. Fetching water and firewood was very risky and dangerous as there was always the risk of snakebites, spiders, bees, scorpions, wasps, itchy grass, etc. On two occasions I was bitten by poisonous snakes while on my way to fetch water and firewood. Both times I almost lost my life, as there was no hospital or medical personnel to treat the snake poison. I can recall drinking my urine after snakebites as it was believed to be an anti-venom.

After completing our individual tasks we were expected to meet our parents and older siblings at the mid-way distance between the farm to our home to assist them with the load they were carrying on their way back home. At the end of each day everyone was exhausted; there was no time to read or do assignments from school. We went to bed late, and woke up early—too early. On Saturdays we spent the whole day on the farm with our parents and on Sundays we went to church in the morning and back to the farm in the afternoon. The only farm tools available at that time were machetes and locally made hoes. Every activity, including felling and clearing trees in the forest, tilling, seeding, weed control, harvesting, and transportation was manually done as there were no other machines available for use.

This was my daily routine until I turned nine. I remember thinking that it was hard, but little did I know that my responsibilities would continue to increase in difficulty and time expenditure. It is important to note that, even today in the twenty-first century, what I had to do is still the daily routine for some kids in the village where I was born.

My Responsibilities at Age Nine and Older

When I turned nine I was integrated with my older siblings whose morning activity was waking up at three o'clock to transport food items from the farm to our home. Other activities included transporting items from home to the weekly market place, working on the farm and babysitting. Food items and animals that were for sale were transported to the market at least four days per week. The food items we transported had been harvested during the harvest season and stored at the farm. There were no houses on the farm to store the harvested food items and storage was usually under a huge tree. The leaves of trees and banana plants were used to cover the food items. These storage areas became habitats for small mammals, spiders, scorpions, and many other animals. Snakes also visited the storage areas to trap and prey on small mammals.

When I started waking up at three o'clock in the morning to help in the food transportation process it was not easy for me at all. I can remember actually falling asleep while walking during the first few weeks of my new work schedule. It was terrifying and I thought this was just not for me. If I'd had a place to escape to I would have done so.

Access to the farm was through very narrow footpaths covered with grass. In the night the grass was covered with dew, which made it slippery. Moonlight and bush lamps were the only sources of light in the night. We usually lost the bush lamplight either due to rain, wind, or someone slipping and dropping the lamp. By the time we arrived at the farm everyone was soaked wet by the cold dew hanging on the grass along the bushy footpaths. On the days that we lost our bush lamp we would load the food items to be transported home in total darkness. It was very tough to make our way home as the footpath was so dark, slippery, and difficult to trace. We kept falling, rolling, and even lost our load at times, especially when the hill slopes were steep.

This activity was done every day Monday through Friday. The only days we slept till six o'clock were Saturdays and Sundays, as these days were designated to work on the farm. But if the weekly market date fell on a Saturday or Sunday, we woke up at four o'clock to transport items to the market. Looking back now, this backbreaking daily schedule may have contributed to my father's early death at age sixty-five—as well as the fact that he was bitten in the night several times by poisonous snakes and spiders. He survived at the time, but it probably added to the toll taken on his body.

On Saturdays we left for the farm at eight o'clock in the morning and spent the whole day on the farm, returning home at seven o'clock in the evening. During the planting season we spent Saturday nights at the farm, sleeping in little temporary tents. Sometimes it rained and strong winds destroyed our tents in the middle of the night. On Sundays we went to church in the morning and immediately after church service we went back to the farm to work the rest of the day. This was our routine—we humans were substitutes for tractors used in tilling and trucks for transportation.

This routine was not unique to my family—it was a common practice for survival in the entire society. The situation of some families was even worse. Most families, including mine, could not afford clothes and shoes to wear. Most children only had an opportunity to wear new clothes and shoes on Christmas or New Year's Day. Some children could only eat rice on Christmas or New Year's Day. Rice was highly valuable and many families could not afford it. The good thing about this situation is that each family understood it was the only way to survive. Parents and children worked together as a team to support one another. Children did not know anything about children's rights, nor about abuses. Parents had the freedom to bring up their children in a responsible way without fear of being prosecuted for bullying or child abuse. No one interfered with family issues. Children respected their parents and understood that there are consequences for disobedience. They understood that corporal punishment was a corrective measure. Children equally understood that rights, if any, came with responsibilities. Despite the hardship, there was harmony and commitment for "relative survival" in most of these families.

Schooling was such a scary thing as the teachers were strict and ready with corporal punishment every time something went wrong. Each school day I was beaten several times for coming late to school, not completing my assignment, failing mental sums, and many other reasons. Sometimes I spent the whole day in school but didn't learn anything because I would either be taking care of or cleaning up after my younger sibling or I would be exhausted and falling asleep. With all these struggles I managed my way to class seven in primary school, equivalent to grade seven in North American elementary education standards. In class seven, which was the final class of primary school, each pupil was required to sit for two examinations. The Government Common Entrance Examination (GCEE) was an assessment aimed at selecting successful pupils for secondary school. The examination had three grades: grade A was the best, grade B was average, and grade C was considered failure. Those who succeeded with an A grade were admitted into public and prestigious secondary schools and those with grade B were admitted into some privates and mission schools. The second examination was the First School Leaving Certificate (FSLC), which was intended as proof of successful completion of primary school education. This was significant because it was the minimum requirement requested by some employers prior to offering employment.

When it was time for me to register for the above two examinations my classroom teacher and the headmaster did not want me to sit for the exams. The headmaster was not sure I would pass the exams and my teacher was very sure I would not make it. They were afraid my participation in the exams would lower the percentage score of the school. In those days teacher assessment was based on their students' average percentage obtained in the GCEE and the

FSLC examinations. In the previous year my school had 100 percent in the GCEE and eighty-five percent in the FSLC, and there was a strong motivation to keep this up. My teacher was so concerned about his reputation that he did everything possible not to register me for the exams.

A big debate went on and on between my father and the school authorities. My father insisted and I was registered for the two examinations against the will of my teacher. When the results were published, I passed the GCEE in B grade and failed the FSLC. Most of my friends passed in grade A and were enrolled in prestigious public schools. I went through the interview process for two grade B schools and obtained admission for one. My father managed to enroll me in a mission school called Presbyterian Secondary School Batibo (PSS Batibo). The tuition was comparatively very high and we had no money. As I was getting ready for secondary school education we had no choice but to work even harder on the farm.

CHAPTER TWO

My Life in Secondary School

After my enrolment into Presbyterian Secondary School Batibo a list of school supplies and requirements was handed to my dad. Some items that I can remember were two pairs of uniforms, a bucket, broom, a box, or suitcase, a few pairs of pants and inner wear, two pairs of shoes (one black and one brown), one machete, books, pens, pencils, etc. My father didn't have money to afford all these items so he decided to be creative. He had been a tailor by profession before becoming a subsistence farmer, so he decided to buy some pieces of cloth and sew the uniforms himself. He didn't recognize that with changing times, the profession of tailoring had evolved and his way of sewing was outdated. Also, since he was so short of money, he could only afford a small piece of cloth. The piece of cloth was just enough for one shirt for my size, but instead he used it to sew two shirts. Then there were the other items—my school suitcase or box was an old one used by my older sister five years earlier. My broom and bucket were also very old—they'd previously been used at our house. Every other item we gathered, apart from the uniform, was just old stuff picked from the house or other relatives.

As a tradition in the mission schools, all first-year students were expected to be in school one week before the regular school opening day. This was so we could familiarize ourselves with the school environment. We were also expected to clean up the school campus. On the school resumption date for new students my father didn't have enough transport fare for someone in the family to accompany me to school, which is what most families did. The school was in another village far away from our home. I was only thirteen years old at the time and usually parents with cars would drop off their children and those without cars would at least accompany their children to school by public transport. This was not possible in my case, so my father managed to drop me off at the public transit station. When he dropped me off, he gave me 1500 Central African francs (about four dollars) as "leaving allowance" for the whole term. I got onto the thirty-year-old bus with other new students and it took us about three hours to get to school.

When we arrived at the school there was one teacher standing by to receive and distribute the new students into various dormitories. When the driver started offloading the bus, the teacher saw my old box and other used items, he said to the driver, "Please do not offload that old box here, today. I'm receiving only the new students. All other students are not allowed here until the school reopening day." Everyone in the bus started laughing, as they knew the old items were that of a new student. I was so ashamed and this was just the beginning. I started feeling very inferior. The driver finally explained to the teacher that the items were those of a new student.

The teacher questioned, "Who is this new student?" The driver pointed at me and he came closer to me and asked, "Are these really your items?"

I responded, "Yes sir."

He said, "Take your items and follow me." I picked up my old box and followed him. He took me to a dormitory and said, "This is your dormitory and that is your bed."

The next day, there was an inspection of all school requirements and supplies. Each student was required to wear one pair of their uniforms and display the other pair and all other required school items for inspection. Little did I know that my two pairs of uniforms were all under-sized, as I didn't even measure them at home. After taking a shower, I put on one pair of the uniforms, but it didn't fit. I tried the second pair and it was the same. The shirts were too short, just hanging above my navel. My pants were also too small and too short making it impossible to tuck in my shirt. When the inspection team came around, it was sad news for me as my list was not complete and they also had to keep telling me to tuck in my shirt. I was beaten with the cane several times. I cried and cried but it was impossible to tuck in my shirt.

It took me a long time to partially integrate as I was behind in almost everything. Considering that I grew up in a farm environment, I knew nothing apart from fetching water, gathering firewood, and transporting food items. I was mocked by everyone, every day. By mid-semester, one student who had three pairs of uniforms offered to sell one pair to me. The price he wanted was double my pocket allowance. I pleaded to pay half of the amount and to complete the balance by next semester. My hope was that my father would provide me with additional pocket allowance. He finally agreed to this arrangement. Now I had one shirt to wear five days a week.

Before the end of the first semester I was very frustrated and disappointed. I planned to go home during vacation and never return to school. Then, on the last day of school when I was waiting to receive my report card, my classroom teacher informed me that the principal wanted to see me. I was so scared and instead planned to sneak into the bus immediately after receiving my report card. After all, my plan was never to return to that school or any other school. Why did I need to see him? It would be comfortable for me to stay in the village and work on the farm with my parents. Unfortunately for me, as I was waiting in the classroom to receive my report card, I saw the principal standing in front of the classroom door waiting for me. Immediately after I was given my report card he said, "Stanley, come meet me outside." The rate of my heartbeat increased dramatically. If there had been an open window or another door for me to escape through I would have done so. However, I went to meet him outside of the classroom and he said, "You are such a good student, Stanley. I'm surprised that you did well in your exams considering your situation. I have written this letter for you to give to your parents. You see, if your parents are able to provide what you need in school, you can perform extremely well. Have a safe journey home and enjoy your holiday. I hope to see you next semester."

These words were so motivating and my heart was encouraged. On my way home I reflected over and over on the words of the principal. When I got home, I handed the letter and my report card to my father. As he read the letter, tears began to run down his cheeks. He immediately left the letter and the report card and rushed to his room to cry in private. I could hear my mother comforting him and encouraging him to be strong. It was hard for my mother to understand what was going on since she could not read. In the letter my principal explained the challenges I had gone through and what a great student I was despite all that. He also said I could do much better if basic items were provided to me.

During that vacation we worked on the farm even harder and transported more food items to the market. The problem here though was that prices of food items were extremely low. Ninety-nine percent of the population was dependent on agriculture and supply was significantly higher than demand. Only a few people from the city were buying food in the village market and there were several village markets for them to buy from. Because most of the food items transported to the village market were perishable, they either sold for very little money or had to be thrown away as they began to rot. All the money we saved during that vacation was not enough to even pay for my tuition and buy the school requirements. I did manage to get another pair of uniforms and a few new supplies, however, there was definitely no pocket allowance for me this time, so I had no money to pay the balance I owed to the student who had sold me a uniform last semester. When I returned to school I approached this student and explained to him that I was not in possession of any money to pay for the uniform. I proposed returning it to him but he did not want it back as he came with another new pair. But, fortunately for me, he agreed to something that I was able to offer. I had a very big bag of *garri*, which is ground and fried cassava, and he wanted half of it instead of the money. I gave it to him and he was extremely happy—it was a great trade!

Not long after that he became my good friend and we shared most of our items together. He was from a rich family and grew up in the city so he usually had some cash to spend. I was from a poor family and grew up in the village, but at least I usually had assorted food items in my locker. As our friendship grew we gave each other duplicate copies of our locker keys. He could open my food locker and take whatever he'd like and I could enjoy whatever biscuits or cookies he had in his. This friendship was truly a significant turning point for me; I became more confident and began to enjoy school much more. I finally had a friend I could count on and one that was always there to help, especially with things that were new to me. To top it off, both of us did extremely well in the exams, which allowed us to move to the second year. During vacations my father allowed me to visit my friend in the city for a two-week stretch. The intent was to give me a chance to learn about city life and the types of possibilities that existed as per the recommendations of the school principal.

At the end of the second year I returned home only to find my father critically sick. He could not drink water nor swallow food of any type; he would vomit if he tried to eat anything. This went on for a long time and there was no money to take him to a good hospital for diagnosis. When he finally saw a doctor, he was referred to a specialist located in another province far away from our home. Financially it was not possible for him to go see this specialist.

Another hindrance was language barrier—the town where the specialist was located is French-speaking. Also, there wasn't enough money to afford the projected bills of the specialist.

My father returned home in a desperate state without treatment and he continued to vomit each time he tried to eat or drink. After some time he went to another hospital and met a doctor who examined him without the use of an x-ray. It was determined that the cause of vomiting was a blockage in his intestine. The doctor advised my dad to try and gather some money and get ready for an operation in which the blocked part of the intestine would be cut off. My father returned home with the sad news. Fortunately, he was able to borrow money from friends and relatives to go for the operation. We were all sad but hopeful that he could get well after the operation. However, this was not the case, his condition remained the same after the operation and he became weaker and weaker as each day passed. Throughout my father's lengthy health challenges, he continued to be concerned not about himself but about my education. I was in form three at the time and he'd speak to friends and relatives and ask them, "Please support Stanley in school in case I die. Don't let him drop out. That is the only favour you can do for me."

I can remember some people who got very frustrated with my father's statements and would question, "What type of man are you? Are you thinking about your health or your child's education? Don't you see that there are many people in the village who haven't gone to school but are doing just fine?"

The situation became worse and my father was not able to do anything for himself, let alone talk of supporting me in school. My mother became the only person we relied upon for everything we needed. She started working on other people's farms for payment to support us in school and also to support my father during the tough times. This was extremely hard on her and I saw my mother grow older and weaker each day. Then came the magic moment in my life as I thought of a way to keep my father happy and to reduce the stress on my mother. It seemed the only thing that made my father happy was for me to continue with my education. I brought a proposal to my father and mother asking them to permit me, during the holiday period, to go to work in other provinces where there were large farms or plantations. Through this I would be able to work for my tuition and school needs. They both reluctantly accepted and prayed to God to watch over me wherever I went.

At the beginning of each summer holiday period I went home just to greet my parents and also to receive their blessings before going to provinces where I could find work. With their blessings and the motivation to keep my father happy, I became very productive at work and was able to get enough for my tuition and some important school needs. The jobs that I did were all hard labor and were paid based on output. Some included manual harvesting of coffee and cocoa, extracting and collecting natural latex from rubber trees, clearing forest for potential plantations with a machete, and harvesting palm nuts. Despite my young age, short height, and small frame I could do all these things to the surprise of many people. In one circumstance I applied for a contract to clear three hectares of a rubber tree plantation. The contract manager did not want to give it to me because he thought I was so small and too young for the job. I pleaded and pleaded and he decided to test my ability with another portion of the forest. He assigned the area to me and told me, "I'll give you three days to complete this project. I'm not sure you can meet the deadline, but if you do I'll assign the three hectares of rubber trees to you."

The next morning I woke up at four o'clock in the morning and took my machete along with a large loaf of bread, some sugar, and a gallon of water. I arrived on site and started work at six. By six in the evening that day the forest was fully cleared and my assignment was completed. I went back to the camp totally exhausted. Early in the morning of the next day I went to inform the contract manager that I was indeed finished. When he saw me coming, he spoke up quickly before I had a chance, "I knew you would not be able to complete that portion. If you cannot complete that smaller area, how can I assign the three hectares to you?"

I responded by saying, "It's already done, sir!"

He was shocked and did not believe me, even for a second. He said, "I don't like people who are not serious." I told him that I was very serious but he responded with, "Okay I'm taking you there on my bike right now and if that portion is not completed I'll never assign any more work to you." When we arrived he saw that it was perfectly cleared, even more than he expected. He asked: "Did you do this by yourself or did some people helped you?"

I answered by saying, 'I had no family or friends who could help. I was by myself and did all the work alone." Then I questioned him, "Who do you think could actually help me?"

He shook his head and said, "This is almost impossible. It is a miracle!"

He then took me to the three hectares of rubber trees he had promised. He asked if I was going to start that same day or the next. I told him I would prefer to start the next day. Before I left he showed me another three hectares of rubber trees adjacent the one assigned to me and said, "Those three hectares over there have been assigned to two brothers who are also starting tomorrow. You will have some others working close by."

The next morning I left at four o'clock with the usual—my machete, loaf of bread, sugar, and gallon of water. I started work at six o'clock but the two brothers could only arrive at ten o'clock that day. They chatted with me for a few minutes and then went to work. As I was working I could see them taking numerous breaks. At about four o'clock that afternoon I saw them heading home while I continued until six. The next morning I again started work at six and worked my normal twelve hours; they arrived about ten-twenty and left at about three-thirty. Consequently, in two weeks I was able to complete the three hectares while the two brothers were still lagging behind. The very moment I completed the job and started moving towards the main road I saw the contract manager coming to inspect the progress. According to him he expected the job to take a minimum of one month. When he saw that the whole portion was completely cleared he ran toward me and gave me a hug. At that time he also saw that my right palm was bloody from numerous blisters and he offered some sympathy.

Following this the manager called the two brothers in and said, "How can this boy complete his portion before the two of you?"

One of the brothers responded, "We don't know. We think he is using black magic."

The contract manager was so frustrated with that response and said, "This is your last job so long as I'm contract manager in this company!" He took me to his house, used his first aid supplies to clean my bleeding palms, and gave me good food to eat. I became his best worker and in return each holiday he made sure there was a contract reserved for me.

This helped me pay my tuition and my father was more than pleased. My mother was still supporting me in school but her burden was greatly reduced. With all this hard work and support from my mother, I managed my way through secondary school, a grade ten equivalent. As I was contemplating what to do next, my father approached me and encouraged me to go to high school, the equivalent of grades eleven and twelve in Canada. He said, "I know you can make it without anyone's support. I'd like to see you earn a degree and become a pastor or a doctor." This was a challenge to me as I was not sure I could make it. However, I enrolled in a high school and started studying with plans to work during holidays.

The first holiday arrived and I immediately took off to meet my friend the contract manager and secure a job. When I arrived there, however, it was all bad news for me. My friend had retired and all of the work had been subcontracted to another company. There was no job for me, and on top of that I had no money for transport fare to another province or even to go back home. I was literally stranded for two weeks doing nothing, surviving in the hands of some good Samaritans. May God bless all of them, wherever they may be.

One morning I saw the company director talking to a group of workers. I took courage and approached him. When I moved closer towards him with a machete in my hand he stopped talking to the workers, turned towards me and asked, "What do you want, young man?"

I responded, "A job, sir."

He asked, "Are you a regular worker here?"

I responded: "No sir, I'm a student looking for work."

"Have you worked here before?" he continued.

"Yes sir, I did a lot of contracts for your contract manager who just retired."

He questioned, "What is your name?"

"It's Stanley."

"Okay. I heard that you are a serious worker. Unfortunately, all the student jobs have been subcontracted. However, I will still find you some work this holiday. But don't count on it next holiday—just don't come here at all."

I quickly responded, "Thank you sir. Thank you very much!"

He instructed one supervisor to include me in his team. So I joined a team of workers responsible for the extraction and collection of natural latex from rubber trees. Unfortunately, during my second week of work I sustained a serious injury to my leg. My supervisor carried me on his bike to the company health care unit for treatment. Surprisingly, the nurse in charge refused to dress up the wound on the grounds that I was not an employee of the company. I believe it was their company policy. There wasn't another health care unit nearby and I didn't have money for transport fare to a different town for treatment. Two days passed and by this time I realized it was no longer possible for me to continue working with my injury. So the next morning I approached the company accountant requesting payment for my two weeks that I had already worked so that I could go treat my wound. He told me, "You'll have to wait for the next payday which is two weeks away."

I pleaded, but to no avail and for two gruelling weeks I was lying in the camp in pain, waiting anxiously for payday. When it arrived I received my little pay envelope and boarded a bus for the closest town to my village. I was on the bus for about five hours and I vividly remember the other passengers in the bus were not very comfortable with the unpleasant smell of my wound. As soon as I arrived I went directly to the hospital. The nurses had to cover their nostrils before attending to me. They told me, "The wound needed stitches, but it is too late for stitches." However, they dressed it well and administered an anti-tetanus injection.

From here, I went home and it was all sadness in my family for some days. It was only three weeks to school reopening now but luckily my mother and father successfully borrowed money from friends and relatives to ensure that I went back to school. I must mention that at this point, two of my siblings were in secondary school and the rest were in primary school. My parents did a good job of borrowing money for our school needs. I truly must thank all our kind and generous friends and relatives. Some of the money borrowed could only be paid back after many years when I started working. What a long wait and how patient they were.

My life in high school was equally tough financially as I did not have any regular contract work scheduled during my breaks. So during those holidays I travelled from one part of the country to another in search of work. Sometimes I found work and sometimes I didn't. In the end I was successful in high school and I was ultimately happy and proud of myself. My father said to me, "One more step to go and you will be whatever you want to be. I was not able to do what you have done. One day, the son of a poor man shall earn a degree."

I was touched by his words. But at the time I kept wondering why he loved education so much and what motivated him to push me so hard. My father was barely educated himself, a grade three dropout, and all around him in the village that's all he really saw in his fellow man. But over time I understood that he believed education was the key to a successful life, even though he could barely read and write basic English.

Even with his low-level reading he worked his way through the Bible—at the time it was the only book available to him. He mastered the Bible and became a lay preacher in church. Some people who met him for the first time thought he was an actual ordained minister because of his extensive knowledge of the Bible. What an accomplishment for my father. His continuous persuasion and love of knowledge led me into my university education.

CHAPTER THREE

University Education

With words of encouragement and motivation from my father I decided to enrol in a university. At this time there were about five universities in Cameroon located in different provinces. Four of these universities were located in the French-speaking part of the country; none were located in my province of origin. The only English-speaking university was located in the southwest province, which is even farther away from home than some of the French-speaking ones. After careful consideration and in consultation with my family we agreed that enrolling in the closest French-speaking university would be the best option. I submitted an application for enrolment, which was accepted.

As I was planning to go to the university, Bridget, who was my girlfriend, informed me that she was pregnant. We had a serious discussion and decided to get married on a future date since there was no money at that time. We discussed with our parents and they accepted the proposal. A few weeks prior to my departure for school, Bridget moved and started living with my parents.

On the school reopening date, popularly known in French as *la rentrée scolaire*, I boarded a bus with all of my school requirements to my university of choice. A that time, I neither spoke French nor understood it. The bus driver dropped me at the university junction. My first obstacle started immediately. I needed a taxi or a two-wheeled trolley—commonly called a "hand truck" in Cameroon—to transport my supplies to the university campus. The only word I could remember in French was *bonjour*. I stood at the university junction for over an hour trying to construct a sentence in French that someone could understand. Fortunately for me, after some time I saw a young man coming and I approached him and said, "Bonjour!"

He stopped and responded, "Bonjour."

I then said, "Je... je..." The other words to complete the sentence were just not coming to me. He immediately asked, "Are you Anglophone?" meaning, "Are you English-speaking?"

I said, "Yes, sir."

He said, "I'm Anglophone too."

What a relief it was for me. I took a deep breath, could hardly believe it, and again asked, "So you are Anglophone?"

He said, "Yes."

I told him I needed help to get a hand truck or taxi to transport my items to the university campus. He was fluent in French and it took him no time to hire a hand truck for my items and he assisted me in transporting the items to the dormitory. When we got there, I realized that he was living next door to me and in the same faculty. What luck! We quickly became very close friends.

It did not take long for him to know how poor I was. I was constantly borrowing his textbooks to do my reading assignments. Then after a few months he realized that I was unable to pay my rent as the university authorities constantly harassed me out of the room. One evening he called me into his room and had a serious discussion with me. He wanted to know why I couldn't afford textbooks or rent. I explained everything to him and he was extremely sympathetic. Being a very kind person, he told me, "Next semester, if you want you can come stay in my room. If both of us contribute to the rent of one room you may save enough money to buy your books."

He also said "My father has a large coffee farm, about twenty hect-ares, where many people work. If you want you can come with me during holidays to work for my father. That may give you enough money to pay your share of the rent and afford school needs."

I was humbled after hearing these words and very grateful. It gave me hope that some of my financial stresses might be reduced. At the end of the semester, he provided me their home address, which was in another province. First of all, I went home to my parents and explained the great employment opportunity to them before leaving to join my friend. When I arrived at his home he introduced me to his father and the entire family. It was a polygamous home with many wives and children. I felt very fortunate, as the entire family was very friendly and kind to me.

On the coffee farm there were numerous types of jobs to be completed, ranging from weed control (by clearing them with a machete), harvesting coffee, and harvesting other crops that were part of his mixed farming. In the first week his father tried me in all the jobs to see which one I was best suited to. During the second week he told me, "I'd like you to do coffee harvesting because you really do a good job." I told him I was prepared to do whatever he wanted. So he assigned me to coffee harvesting.

For every seventy-five kilogram bagful of coffee that I harvested I was going to be paid 500 francs, equivalent to about one dollar. Each day I was able to harvest eight bags to earn 4,000 francs, or about eight dollars. He was so pleased with my performance and told me, "Stanley, do you know you have broken a record here? No one has ever harvested eight bags of coffee in a single day. The highest has been seven bags."

The third week, after my harvesting record remained consistent, he told me, "I'm going to make you a supervisor, Stanley. Each day you will confirm the bags that other workers harvest. This does not mean you will stop harvesting. You will continue with your normal harvesting and at the end of the day you will confirm the work of these other workers for an additional 500 francs a day." This was great news to me and implied 4,500 francs, about nine dollars, each day. This was the first time in my life that I actually made enough money during the holidays that I was able to pay my tuition and afford most of my school needs.

School resumed and my friend and I returned to the university together. We shared a room and were able to get along very well. We both had a good academic semester. Before the end of the semester my friend's father sent a letter requesting me to accompany his son for vacation. I was excited and at the end of the semester I told my friend I would first of all go home to greet my parents and then travel later to meet him. We agreed and departed for the holiday.

When I got home, my father was critically ill. When he saw me, a weak smile came across his face and he tried to get up from his sickbed, but that was not possible. I went closer to him and shook his hand. The first thing he told me was, "I am a happy man today because I've watched you grow responsibly. If I die, I do not have any regrets because you are smart and will certainly know what to do." He stretched his hand to his bed cupboard, picked up a matchstick, and said to me, "Take this is the light of my household and family that I've given to you. Take good care of it." Tears formed in my eyes and began to fall down my cheeks and he said to me, "Are you not thankful that you have grown up and are now studying at the university before I'm about to die? What about some of my friends who did not live long enough to see their children grow up as you are?" I continued crying and he became frustrated and stopped speaking for the rest of the night.

The next morning, I brought in a nurse to take a look at his condition, as there was no nearby hospital and certainly no money to take him to a hospital in the city. The nurse assessed his condition and administered intravenous medication. There was some improvement the following day and then he said to me: "How I wish you were born earlier. Then you'd have some money to take me to a big hospital and then—who knows? Three weeks ago I was discharged from the hospital because I was unable to afford the bills."

I felt sorry for my dad but there was nothing I could do. Even today when I think of these words of his I feel bad because his story might have been different if he had been taken to a good hospital. A few days passed by and there were signs of improvement. Unfortunately, I knew I needed to leave for work soon so I could pay for my tuition and school needs. I planned to leave the next morning but at about one o'clock my mother knocked at my door and said to me, "Your father is very sick again." I went to his bedside and found him in serious pain. Everyone at home gathered in his bedroom and prayed. The next morning I decided not to leave for work as planned.

In the afternoon of that day he called me and said, "There is no money in this house and it appears there is not enough food also. Why don't you and your siblings get a hand truck to transport some food items from our farmhouse to here? If you do that, we can have some food at home and may be able to sell some on the market day to at least have a small amount of money at home."

Little did I know this would be his last statement to me. What a way of saying goodbye! I went out and got a hand truck and headed to the farmhouse together with my wife, who was with me at that time, and my younger sister. We loaded some bags of food items into the hand truck. Before we got home it was already nightfall. My mother was standing right at the door waiting for us. As we arrived home, she beckoned for me to come immediately. As I was moving toward her, she diverted the attention of my younger sister to go do something else. My wife accompanied me as my mother took us to my father's bedroom. She opened the door of the room, my eyes were immediately focused on the bed and the first thing that came to my mind was that my father might have already died. I went closer, touched him, and listened, but I could not feel nor hear any sign of life.

I started crying and shouting but my mother covered my mouth and said, "Listen to me now! This is not the time to cry. Remember what your father told you. There is a lot to be done and you can't do that if you are crying. Do what is important now and there will be time for you to cry the way you want to later."

This was my first experience with a death in the family. My mother said to my wife and me, "I'll need the two of you to assist me in everything I do." So under her direction we carried his corpse off the bed, washed, oiled, dressed, and displayed my father in the sitting room. It was a tough job, and after quite some time it was completed and my wife and mother burst into tears and began crying. I immediately joined them. Neighbours heard the loud crying and came to our house to join us in mourning my dad. We cried all night.

During this time I kept wondering how we were going to bury him. There wasn't any money for a coffin and I kept saying to myself what a disgrace for my dad to be buried without a coffin. Early the next morning, I went to a radio station located in the city to pay for an obituary announcement. As news circulated about the death of my father, one of my uncles came forward to provide a coffin for his burial. We mourned him for months.

I was unable to work for my tuition and school needs during that time. One month after school resumed, I was still unable to return to school. Then during the second month, my famous friend at the university sent a letter addressed to my sister who lived in the city at that time. He was unable to write me personally because there was no postal address in the village making it impossible to deliver any mail. In the letter he wrote, "Please inform Stanley that we are doing laboratory practical sessions now and exams have been scheduled in three weeks."

Before the information got to me, it was already two weeks past the dates he had outlined. I broke down and wept after receiving this information. My mother said to me, "We have to do whatever it takes for you to return to school. This is the only thing that will please your father wherever he is." She was able to borrow some money and my wife gave me a little money from her own pocket. This was just enough for transportation and rent for one month.

I arrived at the university and the examination timetable was already posted on the notice board—exams were in five days. When my friend saw me, he was very sad for me and showed me the sympathy I needed for my father's passing. He was very kind with his words. Shortly afterward he provided me with some course material and paid the cost of photocopying notes gathered from some classmates. I immediately immersed myself in studying day and night. I locked myself in the room to read exclusively.

During the first examination, I was pulled out of the exam room for not completing my tuition. I was very emotional and went to the Dean of Studies to explain my situation. After I explained the traumatic passing of my father, luckily he said, "I actually heard that death announcement over the radio. I'm going to issue you a note that will allow you to sit for all your exams this semester. But you must pay your tuition before the next semester." I was glad and thanked him for helping.

Then I sat for the exams and when the results were released I learned that I had passed in all the subjects except two. The subjects that I failed were those with practical exams that I had missed. In this university, practical exams were twenty to thirty percent of the final mark, so it was almost impossible to miss practical lessons or exams and succeed in the final assessment. My friends and classmates could not believe my results from just a short period of studying. Even I was surprised, and I thought some super power may have been looking after me. However, I attributed the success to intensive reading and concentration.

At the end of this semester I went home as usual to see my family before going to work for my tuition and school needs. I spent one week at home with my family and when it was time for me to leave my wife decided to leave our son with her mother and accompany me. Even though I wanted her to stay at home, she said, "You know you need tuition for two years, last year and this year. You may not be able to earn that amount by yourself before school resumes. If I go with you, both of us will work together and it will be easy to get the amount you need. You may think that it is hard work for me but I'd rather do the hard work to make sure you succeed in your education."

Eventually, we went together to my friend's village to work on the coffee farm. It took us more than half a day travelling by bus. The next day when I was leaving to begin harvesting coffee I told my wife to take a rest for that day after the long travel. She refused and accompanied me to the farm. When we got there I trained her briefly on the procedures of coffee harvesting. We then began, using locally designed baskets. That first day was one I'll never forget. Bridget was working close to me for about an hour before I turned around to see how she was doing, but she was not there. I called her name but there was no response. Frantically I began shouting her name but could not hear any sound from her nor could I see her. It seemed the sky was falling out of the world. I started asking questions, "Why God? Why her? Why not me? What am I going to tell her parents?" I thought she might have been injured or attacked by a wild animal, as the farm was located in the heart of the forest. My whole body was shaking uncontrollably and tears were streaming down my face.

There had been just three of us working on the farm that day— the owner and the two of us. The farm owner was nowhere to be found either as I shouted his name to explain what had happened and to ask him if he's seen my beautiful wife anywhere. I just ran up and down the rows, shouting, looking, hoping to see some sort of sign of her, even blood or anything. Suddenly, I came around a corner and bumped into her. She was carrying a full basket of coffee on her head and she immediately looked confused and very worried. She also looked very exhausted. When I saw her I had mixed feelings of happiness, sadness, and inquisitiveness. I was very happy that I found her, but at the same time sad that she was suffering through this hard work with me. First and foremost, I wanted to know what had happened to her and why she hadn't answered when I shouted out her name, or if she had indeed been in trouble. I wanted to know what kept her from calling for me to help her. As well, I wanted to know if she was actually okay. Together we determined that she become lost within the large coffee farm and we were both looking for each other in opposite directions. Both of us were tired, discouraged, and decided to stop work for that day.

The next day we gathered courage to go back and continue harvesting. For the rest of the time that we were working there we kept good track of each other so no one got lost. We worked harder and harder each day to make sure we had sufficient money for my tuition and school needs. In fact, it took us a bit longer than planned and we worked two weeks into my next semester. When we asked for our payment at that time, the owner paid us and the amount was just enough to pay my tuition for two years and buy school needs. I said to my wife, "I'll give you part of this money to go home and buy a few items for yourself and our son while I work for a few more weeks to make it up."

Bridget simply said, "We have exactly what we came here for. We must go now. All I need is transport fare to get back home. You must go back to school now so that you don't miss any practical lessons." So we left. She boarded a bus for home while I headed to school.

When I arrived at university I paid my tuition for the previous and current year and was able to buy some important school items. I felt relieved that financially it was all turning out for me this year. Bridget and I had worked so incredibly hard, but it seemed like it had all been worth it. The next thing for me was to get the two weeks of course material that I had already missed. At this time my friend had moved into the department of botany while I was registered in the department of zoology so I could not go to him for help. I approached some other classmates for course material but no one would let me photocopy theirs. I was surprised and confused; I did not know what was going on until I went to another classmate with the same request. He was very honest with me and said, "Do you know why no one wants to help you this time? Because last time you came so late, photocopied the course material of other students and had better results in the end. No one is willing to work for you anymore. However, I'll help you out this time because I know what you are going through." I was shocked and saddened by how the other classmates felt. But I was more than grateful to take his offer. I photocopied the course material he provided and was present in school for the rest of the semester.

It turned out to be a good semester as I succeeded in all the subjects this time. For the rest of my time at the university it continued the same way—I worked for my tuition and school needs during holiday periods. But I learned a very important lesson that year and would do everything possible to have perfect attendance each semester right from the first day that school resumed.

During my last semester at the university coffee prices had fallen sharply and my friend's father did not have any jobs for students. His large family could handle the few jobs he had. I borrowed some money through my mother to do some business. My intention was to buy and sell waste palm oil. The waste palm oil was used by some companies to produce soap, commonly called *savon* in Cameroon. It was costly to buy and transport the waste palm oil from production sites to the sales point. I bought some of the waste palm oil and hired a truck and driver to load and transport the waste palm oil to the sales point. On our way to the sales point we were stopped by the police, who wanted a bribe from me. It was almost a tradition for the police to want a bribe if someone is transporting any item for sale. Since I did not have any money for bribe, I was taken and detained in the police station. As I was in the detention room crying and shouting, a miracle happened. A long-time friend of mine who had become an army officer immediately after primary school heard my voice. He was not working at that police station, but he had something to do there at that same time. He was able to recognize my voice even though we had not seen each other for more than ten years. He told the policemen on duty that he recognized my voice. He wanted to confirm if I was who he thought I was, but the policemen would not let him. He called his boss who was a captain in the army to intervene. The captain contacted the police chief and access into the detention room was provided to my friend. He found out that I was actually his old friend. He talked with me and I told him everything that happened between myself and the police officers. He negotiated with the police and I was set free. After selling the waste palm oil I realized some profit, which was enough for my tuition and school needs.

In the end I graduated. What an incredible accomplishment for myself and for my father, my mother, and my wife, who had all helped fund my education in one way or another. Sadly, I was unable to attend the graduation ceremony. Not only did I lack the resources to rent a graduation robe, but I also didn't have any money to organize a graduation celebration. It was a tradition in our culture at that time for every graduating student to organize a party for friends and family. It was disgraceful for a graduating student not to supply some food, drinks, and music for people to enjoy. For these reasons, I was ashamed to be in town and not wear the prestigious graduation robe nor invite friends and family for a party. Before the graduation day I disappeared without letting anyone know my whereabouts. Many people who were not very close to me thought I had not successfully graduated. I remember one particular person from my village who had attended the graduation ceremony hoping to see me in a graduation robe. He was working in the town where the university was located. Unfortunately, he did not see me and was disappointed. When he traveled back to the village, he told my mother and other people in the village, "I'm not sure Stanley graduated. I was there and did not see him nor did I hear any mention of his name." My mother was quite disturbed, but by the time she mentioned it to me I was in possession of my graduation certificate. I proudly presented it to her even though she could not read and I assured her that I was indeed successful and I had attained what my father had wished for so many years: "One day, the son of a poor man shall earn a degree."

CHAPTER FOUR

Life After My Bachelor's Degree

As my life at university was coming to a close, and graduation was in the near future, my hopes were at an all-time high! I thought the toughest part of my life was almost passed. I had dreams of finding a good job and living a better life, just like those I knew who had graduated some years before my time. I imagined myself living in a good house and driving in a good car. Little did I know the toughest challenge was still ahead of me.

In the past, people with university degrees were automatically employed by either the government or in the private sector. But at the time I graduated the economy had taken a turn for the worse. We started hearing about a global economic crisis but it was still hard for me to believe the seriousness and impact that it would have in my personal world. I simply didn't think the crisis could affect my chances. I thought it was just politics as usual.

But I still had some hope in finding a job. I was prepared to pick up any odd job to begin with. At that time in Cameroon job postings for university graduates were advertised over the radio. I bought a small hand-held radio, which I took with me wherever I went. Each day and night I was tuned to the radio listening for opportunities. An entire year went by and I didn't find any type of work related to my degree. During this time I was responsible taking care of my wife and son and times were getting tougher all of the time.

At the start of the second year of job searching, my wife and I decided to start the cultivation of some crops while waiting for a lucrative job. I went to the local market and bought a machete and hand hoe. I used the machete to clear and fell trees in the forest and my Bridget farmed using the hand hoe. The land we farmed had been owned by my late father. We planted a variety of crops including bananas, plantains, cocoyam (taro roots), and some vegetables. We also started another farm of about three hectares where we planted coffee and cocoa. Fortunately, the land was fertile and the crops did extremely well. In the first year we were able to harvest the annual crops and vegetables; the bananas, plantains, cocoa, and coffee were still on the farm. The harvest of the taro roots was so bountiful we didn't have enough space to store our produce. Just like in years past, the only means of transporting the produce was by carrying it on our heads. There were no good roads or vehicles to use at that time and that is still the case even now. It was so disappointing to see most of the produce rot on the farm. The little we transported to the village market was either sold at giveaway prices—ten kilograms of taro roots sold for only 500 francs, the equivalent of one dollar—or was thrown away. The enormous energy and labor that had been wasted was beyond disheartening.

Not long afterward, however, we saw huge bunches of bananas and plantains shooting from our plants. We found some short-lived happiness and hope. It turned out that we were also unable to harvest and transport a good quantity of this produce to the market. Even the few that we successfully transported were again sold at giveaway prices. Frustration and fatigue engulfed us.

I thought I could try something different and once again we tried another strategy. I decided to start harvesting palm nuts and milling palm oil from naturally grown palm trees in my late father's forest. These palm trees were an average of fifteen meters tall and the only known method of harvesting the nuts at that time was to climb to the top of the palm tree by using a rope tied around the waist. In the course of climbing the palm tree both hands were used to hold the rope. A machete was held between the shoulder and the head with the head tilted toward the shoulder to support the machete. This was a very dangerous activity, especially because there was a high probability that the machete would slip or that the rope would be cut off. Many people lost their lives and continue to do so as a result of accidents during this harvesting method.

I was also a victim on several occasions, but the angels of my God were always around to keep me safe. In one circumstance, the rope cut off and I fell from a fifteen-meter height, landing very close to a large rock. Even today I can't understand how and why I survived. I lost consciousness for several hours, lying alone under the palm tree. When I regained consciousness there was blood on my face, hands, and feet. It was extremely hard for me to get on my feet and walk home. There was no cell phone or any other method of communication that one could use at that time. However, somehow I managed my way home, albeit in serious condition.

In another circumstance, while trying to cut and remove a palm nuts cones at the top of a palm tree, I was attacked by a poisonous snake. I fell from the palm tree on rocks and palm fronds. My arm was swollen from the snakebite and I had pain pulsating throughout my body. Again, I survived this attack; I truly believe it was by the grace of God.

Despite these struggles for survival accompanied by pain and stress, I did not find comfort from the people in my community. Before I graduated from the university only three other people from my village in different generations had graduated—all of them had successfully found good jobs. This lead the people in my village to believe that any child who is successful in university will almost automatically find a good job. In my case they started doubting if I honestly did graduate. Some of them insulted me in various ways.

In one instance, I gathered the palm nuts that I had harvested into a big bag weighing about seventy-five kilograms. I carried the palm nuts on my head to transport to the local manual mill site. On my way I met one elderly person who said, "Wow, my son, you are able to carry this much? This must be the consequence of failing exams. At least you are strong enough to succeed in odd jobs even though you could not succeed in the university." In another instance our neighbor's child, who was about nine years old, constantly refused to go to school. When the mother insisted that he must go, he said, 'Why do you keep bothering me? Is education of any value? What about our neighbor Stanley who has gone right through university but cannot find a job?" These two instances and many others made me emotional and very sad both day and night.

Even my wife was getting frustrated and started saying things to me like, "Do you think you can get a job by staying in this village? You are not serious in your job search." Not long from that day it was my mother's turn to express her displeasure of the situation. She returned home one afternoon and wanted to do laundry but she couldn't find the small piece of soap she'd left in her room. It is worth noting that there are no laundry machines in my village. Everyone does laundry by hand. I had used it to wash a few clothes of mine. She was frustrated and didn't know I was lying in my room. She started talking to herself and said, "What a world! A poor woman like me who has given birth to eight children, suffered to bring them up and educate them. Instead of them assisting me with soap, I'm the one assisting them. What am I going to do with my dirty dresses now? It is better for me to just die and stop seeing what is happening. Where is my late husband to come see my situation?" When I heard her say all these things out of frustration, I felt very sorry for her. I got angry with myself and everyone around me as I reflected on it over and over that same afternoon and evening.

A new idea came to mind and I decided to leave our village for another province. All the money I had was just enough to pay a bus fare from the nearest town to that province. I calculated it would cost ten dollars and I had saved exactly that from several months of hard work. The problem was, though, I didn't have enough money for the first leg of my journey. I didn't have the fare needed to get from my village to the nearest town. I didn't ask anyone to help me with money since I didn't want anyone to know that I was leaving. At about four o'clock the next morning I quietly left and started walking to the nearest town. I arrived there at about seven o'clock that same morning and boarded a bus for another province. My wife and mother did not see me in the morning but thought I'd left early for the farm, as usual. When it was nightfall they were worried and started looking for me all around the village. No one had any clue where I was. Family members were very concerned and a search for Stanley went on and on for several weeks

As the bus approached the other province late in the evening I didn't know anybody and was not sure where to spend the night. When the bus arrived at the final stop, a park that was close to the main road, I picked up my little bag and stood by the road. As vehicles drove by I became covered with dust. Many things were going through my mind at that moment. Suddenly and luckily, one of my primary school classmates was passing by and saw me stranded by the side of the road. He approached me and called me by name. I had been in the middle of deep reflection and finally snapped to attention. There, right before me, stood a childhood classmate and friend. He was so happy to see me and asked, "Stanley, where are you going to? I live just close by—let's go to where I live so that you can to take a shower." We went to where he was living and he introduced me to the owner of the house, who was a widow.

The woman was very kind to allow me to shower and she also gave me some food. While eating, the woman looked at me and realized that I was not happy. She began to ask questions, "So where are you going?" I told the woman I was looking for a job and didn't even know exactly where I was going. She asked, "Do you have someone to live with?"

I admitted the truth. "No,' I said, and tears started running down my face.

She felt sorry for me and said, "I can provide you with a room to stay in, but I don't know how you are going to get a job. Your friend is staying with me and helping me to fetch water, split firewood and do other things that I'm not able to do. The same thing will apply to you as long as to you live with us in this house."

I was happy and relieved from some of my stress. When I asked my friend what he was doing for work, he answered that he was a "truck pusher," which means he was transporting items for people in a two-wheel trolley. This job was and still is a degrading job in Cameroonian society. People doing these types of jobs were and are still considered third-class citizens. It was a physical and very dirty job and many people wouldn't do it for a living. Someone else owned the two-wheel trolley that my friend was working with and he paid rent to the owner each day that he used it. I had no other option but to join my friend in his job of transporting items such as fresh fish from the sea site to the camps for drying. Each day we were able to realize 2,000 francs, or about five dollars, after paying rental for the trolley.

During this time, however, a new challenge occurred in my life as I worked with my friend. He was a gambler and unfortunately he introduced it to me. Each day after work, we jointly played a game of horse racing commonly called "*tierce*" in Cameroon. This game required selecting four winning numbers, or horses, out of twenty competing horses in order to win. As with most gambling, we never chose all four of the numbers accurately. Each day we had two or three numbers right but were missing the fourth one for a win. Some days we wasted all the money we worked for in hopes of winning millions. Naturally, this never happened and I became addicted to the game, as did my friend.

After about two months without a win, I got frustrated and started looking for another job and for ways to avoid my friend. By this time I had sent a letter informing my wife and mother of my whereabouts. One day I decided not to work and not to play the game. I must admit it was a tough decision especially not to play the game. The feeling I had was like missing a unique day to win millions. What would my friend think of me in case he won? All these things bothered me all day as I moved around looking for a job. However, I found some comfort in the evening when the results of the game were released and my friend did not win. This encouraged me not to play the game again the next day. As I went around asking people for a job, there was no offer and no information about available jobs. The temperatures were rising, vehicles drove by and I was covered in dust. When it was mid-day with temperatures of about forty degrees Celsius I was exhausted and decided to get shelter under a tree very close to a liquor depot, commonly called "off license" in Cameroon. As I was standing under a tree, a truck loaded with beer, wine, and other drinks came to supply the liquor depot. As I watched the driver and sales person jump out of the truck it occurred to me that the sales person was familiar. I looked closely and he seemed to be one of my secondary school and dormitory mates. He was well-dressed and looked very responsible. I decided to approach him and find out if my eyes were deceiving me. As I moved closer he saw me and shouted my name, "Stanley, what are you doing here?" He hugged me and we sat down and discussed things at length.

I explained my situation and he was so sorry he gave me all the money he had in his wallet—about five dollars. He also provided information about an upcoming recruitment in a company called Tiko Banana Project (TBP) — Del Monte Cameroon. This company was located in another town but very close to where I was. I decided to move to the next town in anticipation of that recruitment opportunity. When I got to that town I decided to go to the company office to inquire about the recruitment requirements. In my mind I was expecting to hear minimum level of education but surprisingly the young man I met told me the only requirement was a new machete and one pair of rain boats.

I thought about for a while, but realized that it was my only option—I could no longer continue with the life I was living, as I was not really getting anywhere. So I went back and purchased a new machete and a pair of rain boats to prepare for the recruitment day. That day I arrived at the recruitment centre and to my greatest surprise I saw several hundred people waiting for about forty general labor positions. When the moment arrived for the recruitment officer to select these forty out of about seven hundred people, I started panicking, especially because I did not know anybody. Recruitment in Cameroon at that time was based on a number of factors: family status and connections, political affiliation, region of origin, and the amount of money one could offer as bribe.

None of these factors were in my favor as I had no money and I came from a poor family. People from poor families had no recognition or connections. The recruitment officer then read a list of twenty-five people who were already recruited—they obviously had either given a bribe or had a referral from an important family member or friend. The remainder of the candidates were now competing for about fifteen positions. After the recruiter was done registering the initial recruits, he announced to the large crowd, "Put up your machetes and pair of rain boots for me to see." There were just a few of us who had new ones so we were selected to complete the required number.

What upset me in this process was that the first twenty-five successful candidates did not have any of the requirements. They played by a privileged set of rules; some were not even present for the recruitment. Even though I was upset, I was not surprised because while I struggled for years without gainful employment, some classmates I had graduated with at the same university, and who had earned even lower grades than I, had been employed. Some of them received a recommendation letter from a famous politician or an important family connection and this was enough to ensure their employment. It didn't matter what grade you had in university or your level of expertise. Any consideration of merit was just written on paper and not put into action.

My first assignment as general laborer was to harvest bananas in a crew or team of five people. The crew leader was called a "cutter" and he was always someone with a lot of experience. New workers like me were called "baggers" and "haulers." The hauling job was very tedious, as one was required to haul twenty-five bunches of bananas from the field to the packing station. This was done by pulling a string of banana bunches on the cableway rollers. Some of the banana bunches were very heavy and some parts of the banana field were hilly, which made it physically very demanding. I did this job for about two months.

Due to high competition in the world market the company needed International Organization for Standardization (ISO) certification to survive competition and continue selling bananas. In order to obtain the ISO certification the company was required to implement standard operational procedures (SOP) specified by ISO. The cutters were required to understand the ISO concepts to be able to respond accurately to the ISO auditors. Most of the crew leaders never went to school and this became a big problem to most of them. Management started looking for crewmembers who could master the ISO concept in order to replace the cutters.

Because I was able to respond effectively to the ISO auditors, I was selected as crew leader for my team. This did not sit well with the very experienced workers and they tried to demonize me each day. They did a lot of research on me and became disappointed to know that I was a degree holder. Some of them said to me, "We hear you are a degree holder? How can a degree holder be harvesting bananas with illiterates like us? If I were you, I'll fall off a cliff for all those years wasted in school. You don't need a degree to harvest bananas." It was humiliating to me but I relented because I had a responsibility to take care of my wife, son, and my mother. My wife did not have a job at this time and was dependent on me. This went on and on each day. Every day I went to bed emotionally exhausted and defeated.

As a harvester I woke up at four o'clock each morning to catch the company truck at four thirty and start work five thirty. Each day's job ended at about six o'clock in the evening. It was depressing to go through all these issues and especially difficult without good food to eat. Each day I grew pale and weaker. One evening I returned from work and sat on a bench in front of the house where I lived. I was so exhausted and tired that I was unable to fetch water for a shower. There was no plan for dinner. All of a sudden and almost like in a dream I saw a lady carrying a child on her back and some items on her head moving toward me. I didn't really care who that could be as I didn't expect any friend or relative. I was already used to my loneliness and could not imagine someone coming to visit. She continued closer to me and began to ask, "Do you know someone called Stanley?" For a few moments she didn't recognize me, but then all of a sudden she realized that I, Stanley, was sitting right there on the bench. At the same time, I realized that this woman was actually Bridget, my wife, and she was carrying our son on her back. We hugged each other and wept together. She questioned me, "Are you sick? Are you okay?"

I told her I was okay but she wouldn't believe me. She stayed with me and I continued doing the hard work as laborer. But now my situation had changed so much for the positive, especially as Bridget could prepare healthy meals for me to eat. As I continued doing that job, and performing well, some of the workers had pity on my situation and said kind words to me. One evening while I was returning to the packing station after harvesting bananas for the whole day someone saw me and shouted, "Stanley, make sure you check the notice board before going home. I think there may be good news for you."

When I got to the packing station I checked the notice board and saw an internal aptitude test advertised for various positions. I submitted my documents to sit for the exams. The documents I submitted included my bachelor's degree. One of the field assistants who was very impressed with my performance and who knew how the system operated saw my degree in the application. He called me in to give me some important advice. He said, "Withdraw the bachelor's degree because that could limit your chances." In a low voice he added, "Listen, the managers do not want to see someone with a degree because they feel threatened." I took his advice and withdrew the degree. I was then allowed to sit for the exams and fortunately I was successful and started working in a specialized position.

While working in this new position I did almost everything beyond their expectations, but most of the managers deliberately refused to recognize my efforts. They kept looking for problems where there were none. I saw hatred without cause. It didn't take long for me to realize the truth in the advice that was given to me about managers not being happy to see people with higher education. Additionally, I saw managers very uncomfortable in my presence. I realized how education could be very powerful and at the same time a crime in the eyes of some people. After working for about four years an announcement from the TBP managing director was circulated asking all degree holders to submit their highest certificates for reclassification. At that time there were about ten degree holders working in various positions, including general labor. All of us submitted our documents with happy faces and with hopes of moving up the ladder. But surprisingly, TBP management took a decision to terminate all degree holders. Termination letters were prepared for all of us who submitted the certificates. Fortunately for me and a few other people, we had been made permanent workers and the company lawyer advised them to withdraw the termination letters for those who were already permanent workers. This is how I survived the diabolical plan against degree holders. All degree holders who were not yet permanent workers were terminated. How on earth can there be progress in any business if talented people are punished and illiteracy is encouraged?

Not long after witnessing this inhumane approach to business there was a sit down strike for all workers. I did not have any idea this was about to happen, not even a hint. One morning I went to the company transit station to board a truck to go to work. When I arrived at the station I saw the whole place crowded and the trucks were all empty. It was then that I realized the workers were striking. Instead of travelling via the work trucks, I paid public transport to go to work that day. I did my job and my boss signed my time sheet. Surprisingly, when management decided to terminate the organizers of the strike, one of the managers included my name on the list and labeled me "ringleader." Then I was issued a query letter. In the letter I was asked to explain why I should not be terminated for being a ringleader in the strike and absent from work on the day of the strike. It was easy for me to respond. In my response I asked whether it was possible for anyone to organize a strike without participating and communicating with others. If I was part of the strike I wouldn't have paid public transport to work. If I was absent from work, my boss wouldn't have signed my time sheet. Fortunately, a copy of my time sheet was enough to prove my ignorance of the strike.

When I presented the facts in my response the company lawyer warned management not to terminate me. I again survived and proved the importance of education. Without my knowledge derived from my education I would not have been able to defend myself. When most of the managers realized how smart I was and how difficult it was to wrongfully terminate me they resorted to shouting at me, just like toothless bulldogs. This attitude was particularly disturbing to me but it did not deter me from furthering my education. While surviving the waves of attack each day, I gradually put up a plan to further my studies in Belgium. Fortunately I was able to obtain admission to do a master's program in Physical Land Resources at the University of Ghent in Belgium.

I borrowed money from the credit union for the visa process, but, unfortunately, my visa application was rejected. I was determined to continue with the process so I again I borrowed money from the credit union and filed another visa application. It was approved thanks to the kindness and generosity of Irene and Ephraim, who provided an affidavit of support.

My next challenge was the fare for the flight. I borrowed additional money from the credit union, but this was not enough for my flight, tuition, and rent. Fortunately, Walters gave me €100 (one hundred euro) to complete my flight fare. For this I am thankful and forever indebted to all these people who played a vital role in the journey of an African child.

CHAPTER FIVE

My Education at the University
of Ghent - Belgium

I arrived in Belgium to do a master's degree program without knowing how to turn on a computer. The only thing I could (barely) do on a computer was to check my emails. Some people will wonder how on earth someone goes through a university and obtains a bachelor degree without knowing how to turn on a computer, which to them is just pressing a button, but nothing is simple when you don't know it. In my time, there were very few computers available in Cameroon and the underprivileged like me could not afford tuition for computer classes. Theses were hand-written and many students actually graduated from the university without knowing anything about computers. I was not the only one.

At the University of Ghent, my very first assignment was in soil physics. I went home and did my assignment neatly on clean sheets of paper. The next morning I happily took my assignment to the instructor who looked at me and questioned, "What is this?" I responded by saying, "It is my assignment, sir." He told me, "You have to do it on a computer and submit it online." I told him I did not have a computer. He was very surprised and told me, "Young man it is not my business if you don't have a computer. Take back your assignment and do it on a computer. I cannot accept handwritten assignments. Know that everything here is done on the computer and you must get one for yourself."

This was just the beginning of frustration and stress on my path. I didn't know what he meant by online. I was on self-sponsor and my funds were very limited, if not lacking. I started wondering how to get money for a computer that I never budgeted for. How to acquire some computer skills was another issue. Due to lack of funds, I was not able to buy a computer for several months. I could only have access to my friend's computer after twelve midnight to try and do my assignments. This strategy was not working very well as my friend would sometimes work on his computer until three o'clock in the morning. I was not able to complete most assignments on time because of not having a computer.

When it was time to write the first test in statistics I was well prepared for the test. This test was to be done on a computer and my friend helped me understand how to draw histograms and other charts on the computer. When I went to write the test it was about responding to questions and representing the various responses into charts and graphs. But something was slightly different. Each student, including myself, was given a diskette to copy all the responses from the computer. This was actually my first day to see a diskette with my eyes. I had never copied information or files from the computer to another device. I had never even heard of USBs or memory sticks, nor did I know what purpose they were used for. Knowing that I was unable to copy the responses of my test to the diskette, I called the examiner and explained to him that my responses were on the computer but I was not able to copy into a diskette. This is how he responded to me: "What have you been doing over the years? You will have a zero if you can't copy your response into the diskette." I sat in front of the computer until every student left. The examiner collected all the diskettes, including mine, which was empty.

When the results were released, I had a zero as he promised. The test counted for thirty percent of the final examination. Before the final examination, I requested an opportunity to redo the test but the instructor told me, "There is no time for that." He continued, "If you want to succeed in this subject, you must be able to obtain at least fifty percent out of seventy percent on the final exam. This is hard and I'm not sure you can make it." I was challenged and decided to work extremely hard for the final examination. When the final results were published, I had fifty-five percent and my instructor was surprised. He told me, "Congratulations. I'm surprised by your results. You deserve some respect."

As I faced numerous challenges, including finances, I decided to work part-time to be able to buy a computer and some school requirements. It was so hard to combine the master's program and work. All students in this program had funding or scholarships, except four students, including myself, who were on self-sponsorship. By the end of the first semester, two self-sponsorship students dropped out of the program. By the end of the first year I was the only self-sponsored student who succeeded to move into the second year. My average was even better than that of some of the funded students. In the second year I continued combining studies and part-time work. It was hard for me to find a thesis topic as most of the professors wanted students to go back to their home countries to collect samples for analysis. This was not a problem for all the other students as their trips and cost of collecting samples was funded. Looking at my financial situation, it was impossible for me to go back to Cameroon for samples collection.

Finally, I found one professor who understood my circumstances and offered me an opportunity to do my thesis with him. Instead of analyzing samples from tropical soil, I analyzed soil samples from the temperate region. My thesis involved intensive laboratory analysis and I spend most of my time, including Sundays, in the laboratory. In the end, despite all the challenges, there was a chance for an underprivileged son of a peasant farmer to also graduate at a master's level. There was a chance for me to put on the prestigious graduating robe of the University of Ghent without paying rental fees. There was a chance for the underprivileged like myself to shake hands and take pictures with the Rector and Dean of a university in a developed country. There was freedom for me to choose not to organize a graduation party and not to be ashamed.

By the time I completed my master's program there was a PhD opportunity. I contemplated accepting the offer, but my family was priority to me at that time. The PhD offer was very attractive with many advantages but this would have meant dropping an immigration opportunity to provide freedom and hope to my children and family. I thought of accepting the offer but it would have been too much for me to handle. My wife had never travelled out of Cameroon. It would have been difficult for my wife and kids to survive in Canada by themselves while I studied somewhere else. I thought it would be stressful for me and for the family. This is how I missed out on this unique opportunity that would have kept my father happy, wherever he is.

Before the PhD offer, I was working full-time in order to raise money for my family's immigration process to Canada. I knew it required a lot of money to sponsor a family of six from Cameroon to Canada. Fortunately, I had the strength to do three jobs in a single day. My first and very important job was with the University of Ghent starting each day at eight o'clock in the morning, working until three. The second job was at Holiday Inn express from four in the afternoon until nine thirty. The third job was with Tower Automotive from ten at night until six the next morning. Each day I had less than two hours of sleep and most of the time I rested in my car between six thirty and seven fifty in the morning. This went on for months and months without actual rest or sleep. My whole system was in disorder and I constantly felt as if something was lacking in my body. For the entire year—365 days—I worked at least seven and a quarter hours every day, including Sundays. I can remember how I lost my balance while walking or riding a bicycle on several occasions. It was hard but I understood there was no relative or friend to help me out financially. I was all by myself, relying on the grace of God to survive. After saving some money I travelled to Cameroon to make arrangements for my family to travel to Canada. When I got to Cameroon circumstances including poor health prevented me from returning to Belgium. We later travelled to Canada from Cameroon.

CHAPTER SIX

My Family Situation in Canada

When we arrived at the Edmonton International Airport on January 21, 2010, two Cameroonian friends were standing by to pick us up. We were accommodated for nine days by the family of Walters. This was a huge help and I could not have expected more. After this period we moved to a rented apartment and started a new life. Before we moved to our apartment a Canadian couple provided us with beds, dressers, pots, and cutlery. As we moved into our own apartment and started settling down my daughter fell sick and her situation became serious. We were running out of money and there was no job yet. I sent out hundreds of resumes but no one ever called back. In 2010 it was really hard to find a job, as the recession was not yet over. I had to pick pop cans and bottles in order to pay some bills. It was a good experience, though.

One day we came across a very kind Canadian woman who became very instrumental in our family. She assisted us in paying our rent ($950) for one month, but when we tried to return the money to her later on she refused. She also helped us with our sick daughter by paying for part of her medications and taking her for medical appointments. She provided bunk beds and mattresses for my children. There is no way I can ever pay back all she did for my family, but I commit her in my prayers and ask my God to bless her abundantly.

Dayspring Presbyterian Church provided immeasurable contributions to my family. The entire congregation provided us with food from the food bank and spiritual and moral support. Individual families from the congregation provided household items to help us settle. God alone is able to reward this type of generosity.

One friend in the United States of America heard about my family's situation and gave us a gift of $200, which we used to buy food. May God also replenish his pockets so that he will be able to help others who are in similar or worse situations.

All the generosity from Canadians and friends is very much appreciated, but even so there were not enough to fill the gap of actually working and receiving a paycheck. Considering my background, I always felt, and continue to believe, that there is dignity when one is able to work and receive a paycheck. It makes a big difference when one is able to manage hard-earned money. It makes one feel responsible to the family and society.

After a couple of months I picked up a security job that paid ten dollars per hour. My wife also picked a dishwashing job for $ 10 per hour. It was hard for me to work in the night. It was my first experience dealing with people struggling with homelessness, drugs, and other crimes. A day before I received my first check my daughter's illness was critical. A doctor had prescribed medication costing over $300 that I was not able to afford. I was not sure that my daughter would survive from her illness. When I received my paycheck it was about $870 and I immediately rushed to the bank to cash the check for my daughter's medication. Surprisingly, the bank told me they were holding the cheque for five business days before cashing. I pleaded and pleaded that the bank should hold the check and provide me with $300 for my daughter's medication, but no one would listen to me. I left with the check and tears started running down my eyes as I walked home.

On my way home I saw another bank and decided to go there and explain my situation even though I did not have an account with that bank. When I got into the bank I saw an elderly woman who quickly realized that I had been crying. Even though I tried to wipe away all the tears, she could still see from by eyes that I've been crying. She asked, "Why are you crying? Come over here." She took me to a little corner and I explained my situation while holding the check. She said, "I know exactly what you are going through and I'll do everything to help you. Just give me a few seconds, okay?" She went away and made a few phone calls and cashed the check for me. I was very surprised, especially as I did not have an account with that bank. I left happily and went directly to a pharmacy where I purchased the medication for my daughter. The medication did not help my daughter but I was happy that I bought her some medication and that her situation was not getting worse because of my inability to buy her medication.

After a few months I went and met the lady who assisted me in the bank and told her I wanted to open an account. She said: "Don't open an account here just because I helped you." I insisted that I open one and today I'm still glad, as she keeps helping me. May her kindnesses be blessed.

As I struggled with the security job and family responsibilities, I was fortunate to receive funding for oil and gas education in a college in Edmonton. It came like a miracle. One morning after my security job shift a colleague with whom I worked offered to give me a ride home. I turned down the offer and boarded a bus. In the bus I picked a *Metro* newspaper in which I saw an advertisement for an oil and gas training program and funding. I got off the bus and took another bus to the college that advertised the course. When I arrived at the college I was told that an entrance exam was required. I was asked to go home and prepare for the exam and to come back to write the exam. I insisted to write the exam there and then. When the exam was marked, I passed and an application for funding was submitted. The application was granted and I started the schooling, still working in the night as security guard. It became apparently impossible to combine the security job and my education and I had to drop the security job.

Due to increasing cost of living, I later picked up an evening cleaning job to combine with the education. Each day, I finished school at five thirty in the afternoon and started the cleaning job at six. As well, I had to pick up my daughter from daycare between five thirty and six. It was stressful but my determination and focus led me through those very difficult moments. As I did my cleaning so well I was assign the responsibilities of cleaning supervisor. I received insults and abuses because a few workers could not see themselves being supervised by a black man. One of the workers even went to my manager and proposed that he would rather do the supervisory job for less pay than being supervised by me. My manager immediately dismissed him from work but I also decided to stop the cleaning job because most of the workers were very unprofessional.

After graduating from the oil and gas program in 2011 life was still very tough for my family and me, but there was hope. The fact that some employers would contact me after receiving my resume was reassuring. This was not the case prior to upgrading my education and skills. With time, I was employed by two subcontracting companies to work at Nova Petrochemical in Red Deer and Suncor in Fort McMurray, respectively. These two jobs gave me hope and courage to strive for better opportunities. In the end I found my dream job with Environment and Sustainable Resources Development (ESRD). This job has changed my life and that of my family, as we are able to live the Canadian dream of mortgaging for a house and paying our monthly bills. Even though I've never had an opportunity to enjoy my life I feel successful. The success is not about me but about my children, who hope to have a good foundation in a land full of opportunities. I'm so glad that my children will never go through the stress and strain I endured throughout my life. They now have the opportunity to study as much as they want and to pursue their dreams without fear of being discriminated against based on family status. They may not be required to bribe before being offered a job, as was the case in my country of birth.

I hope their employment shall be based on merits. They may never need politician(s) or "godfathers" to determine their future. It is up to my children to work hard in school now and become whatever they dream of. I may not be able to do all that Canadian parents do for their children but I'm convinced and hoping that my grandchildren will have the opportunity to enjoy life as other Canadian children. There is still much work to be done, but I feel like celebrating success, especially as I've come from a very long way. It is time for me to publicly say thank you God for your guidance, protection, and blessings. I couldn't expect more because you have blessed me more than I deserve. May you equally bless others who are in similar or even worse situations.

CHAPTER SEVEN

My Wife and Children

My wife was also born in a poor family. However, her circumstances were much better than mine. She equally grew up in the village but had an opportunity to spend much time in the city with some relatives. Bridget and I got married and are blessed with five children, three boys and two girls. Bridget has spent most of her time taking care of our children. Our first son was called Bertrand Neba. Bertrand passed away in 1993 at the age of three. Until today, no one knows the exact cause of his death. All we know is that he had a fever and died in the hospital within two days. Lack of equipment and poorly trained nurses were unable to diagnose the cause of the fever that killed him.

A year after Bertrand's death, Blaise Che Afanwi was born under very difficult circumstances. The meaning of Afanwi is "God given." Bridget endured serious labor pain for about a week during the birth of Blaise. We were transferred to four different hospitals. At each hospital a Cesarean-section was proposed, but Bridget's mother wouldn't accept it. According to her, no one in her family had gone through a C-section. She thought a C-section was just the worst thing that could happen to Bridget. When we got to the fourth hospital, far away from home, the doctor examined Bridget and said, "If C-section is not done within twelve hours, Bridget will die." This was scary. Bridget's mother reluctantly agreed that the C-section could be done. A C-Section was conditionally scheduled for seven o'clock the next morning upon receipt of 80,000 francs (about $200). All the money we had was not up to half of the C-Section fee. I left Bridget with her mother in the hospital and returned to the village on foot to borrow money. It took me eight hours of walking to arrive home at about one o'clock the next morning. When I got home everybody was already asleep. I went to Bridget's father to update him on the situation and to ask for money. Unfortunately, he had no money. I left and went to other relatives asking for money to borrow. By the time I got all the money it was three o'clock in the morning. I slept for two hours and left for the hospital. I arrived at six thirty and realized that Bridget had already given birth at five o'clock. It was all joy and I could hardly remember the labor she endured or the long distance I walked all night long.

When Blaise was two years old, he developed curved legs due to calcium deficiency. This was very serious and we took him to the hospital where he spent three months. One of my younger sisters was kind enough to spend time with him at the hospital.

Claude, Leyget, and Mercy were born under similar circumstance of hardship and poverty. When Bridget was four months pregnant with Claude, she was given bed rest for the remaining gestation period to prevent the possibility of a miscarriage. There were fewer delivery difficulties for Leyget and Mercy relative to Blaise and Claude. However, there was always fear for a potential C-Section.

The society in which Blaise, Claude, Leyget, and Mercy were born has not changed by much—a society that lacks basic life commodities such as potable water, good hospitals, designated play-grounds and parks, etc.

I wish the world would one day come to understand the circum-stances of children born in my village and other poor communities in Africa. Children should have a right to play grounds or facilities no matter where they are born. Children should have a right to financial allowances no matter where they are born. Children should have a right to education and not be left behind because of family status. It is my greatest wish that one day there shall be a genuine movement to end poverty around the world. A non-political movement without borders capable of lifting people out of poverty and reducing the ever widening gap between the poor and the rich.

CHAPTER EIGHT

Strategies to Deal with Difficult Life Circumstances

Difficult life circumstances can originate from many sources. They may begin right from birth; some children are born disabled, some lose their mother during labor, and others never get to meet their fathers for various reasons. In other cases, children's difficult circumstances stem from parental abuse. Then there are children without access to education, families without homes, food, and other basic life amenities. Some people have become critically ill without hope of any treatment and some people are involved in various types of accidents. At times it seems some people have done everything right but still can't find their dream jobs or a job at all. Individuals can be humiliated and discriminated against because of gender, religion, race, opinion, politics, and origin.

Sometimes circumstances arise in people's lives without any prior warning; this can turn happiness into sorrow, hope into hopelessness, dreams into nightmares, solutions into problems, discussions into arguments, love into hatred, peace into war, and savings into debt. Our society refers to such circumstances as "emergencies." Some people are prepared to deal with emergencies in one way or another—they may have emergency funds or family and friends to rely on. But others lack emergency funds and do not have family or friends to support them during such difficult times. Emergency funds are actually a fantasy for many people, especially those who live paycheck to paycheck. In many societies, a high percentage of the population falls within this category. Difficult circumstances are obviously more stressful for those without emergency funds, family, or friends. When unexpected difficulties occur, people start wondering and asking more questions than there are answers for. It has happened to me several times and I can remember asking the following questions.

Why me?

Why was I even born?

What crime have I committed to be going through all these things?

Is there any purpose for me in life?

Where is the God I serve?

Is there really a God?

Is there actually justice in the world?

Is there equality in the world?

Did I ask to be born the way I am?

Did I ask to be born in this region or country that I come from?

Will I ever have a good job?

What about you? Have you at one point in life posed any of the above questions or similar ones? How did you feel when you posed these questions? Did you find any answers to your questions?

Despite diversity in the nature of your difficult circumstance, there is often something common—depression resulting from pain, stress, anger, and hopelessness. I fully understand that there are circumstances in life that are beyond the human scope. I equally believe some circumstances are worth fighting against to regain control of one's life. As someone who has gone through very tough trials, I want to assure you that in hope there are miracles.

There have been times in my life when I gave up hope and contemplated committing suicide. Sometimes I barely survived challenges and regained hope to continue the struggle. Do not let any circumstance define your entire life. Fight back and even if you don't win, others may win because you fought. The heart will be comforted because at least you did something about your predicament. Every fight or competition is not just to win. It is to learn, to reassess, and to make corrections, and this will encourage the heart. The secret of fighting back and taking control of one's life is by understanding the indomitable human spirit, which is in everybody. The human spirit is from God and usually very strong and effective when built on faith and hope. When there is hope, the brain seems to be able to function at a higher capacity and with more clarity and there is a chance for better solutions to problems. Hopelessness, on the other hand, brings anger and other emotions to the forefront, which often leads to poor decisions.

Most successful people in life do not have an easy path or free pass. Life is full of ups and downs. Do not let your downs derail you. Experience in handling difficult situations gives you new skills and confidence. It can help you believe in your ability to make changes and it gives you hope that things can and will be better. Imagine, for instance, a person who has given up hope finding a job. Do you think there will be time and effort devoted in searching for jobs and submitting resumes? Certainly not. It is hard if not impossible to get a job without submitting resumes and attending job interviews. A person who has hope is motivated and committed to keep searching and submitting resumes until a job is found. This principle applies to most situations—without hope it is difficult to be motivated, committed, or to set goals.

Life circumstances can be likened to a competition in which competitors have the goal of winning. Success in every competition comes through commitment and an effective execution of a game plan. It is possible to be successful in life no matter your background or circumstances. Stand up to the challenge with a goal and game plan. Strive to compete and succeed even in difficult circumstances. Even if you stumble or squander the first chance, you may succeed in the second, third, or fourth chance, provided there is a will.

I know it is especially hard to find hope during extremely difficult moments. But when you think about an alternative, it may actually be worse. In fact, just recognizing that things could be worse is an effective coping strategy. Each time I gather courage in a difficult circumstance and say to myself, "Thank God—it could have been worse," I feel better and find hope. My life story above illustrates many examples where I used this strategy.

This is similar to what I learned from my late father. Each time he fell sick he visited the hospital. The purpose of his visit was not to see a doctor nor was it for medical consultation. He went there to see the number of people hospitalized with life threatening illnesses and to feel the pain these patients were going through. According to him, he felt better each time he did this. I think this is a good strategy for most people if not all of us to use. If we recognize that there are always people in worse situations than ourselves, psychologically that gives us more strength to persevere.

Another coping strategy I often used is focusing on the positives instead of reacting to the negatives. An application of this comes when I pray to God. My prayers naturally begin with gratitude for everything I have. As I list all of the things I am thankful for, my blessings are clearly revealed and my spirit is immediately uplifted. I purposely use this coping technique and fully believe that the seeds of resentment cannot grow in a grateful heart, to paraphrase self-help guru Andy Andrews. His quote is, "The seeds of depression cannot take root in a thankful heart." That, too, is true.

Taking responsibility for your situation is key. Think a few minutes and ask yourself what you can do to improve your situation. Reflect on it and talk to a few experienced people who may have some ideas to help. Try to stop blaming the source of your problem because it closes the freethinking mind and lowers the human spirit. Don't expect your country, family, or friends to solve all your problems for you. This attitude brings hatred, negativity, and hinders progress in society. Take responsibility for your situation and hope for the better; this will motivate your spirit. I fully believe that God helps those who help themselves. When you take responsibility for yourself, God will be right there by your side.

Have courage. Listen to God's word. When the Israelites were faced with the huge challenge of crossing the Jordan River and walking through the desert, Moses preached messages of courage. One of the powerful messages is presented in Deuteronomy 31:6: "Be strong and courageous. Do not be afraid or terrified because of them, for the Lord your God goes with you; he will never leave you nor forsake you."

Similarly, King David's Psalm 23 verse 4, "Even though I walk through the valley of the shadow of death, I will fear no evil, for you are with me; your rod and your staff, they comfort me." The lesson from the above verses is about hope, courage, and strength in times of challenges. Even the Israelites, the chosen people of God, faced challenges. Challenges will not last. Those who have hope and are strong and courageous will last. The Israelites overcame all their challenges through courage and trust. The same can be true for all of us who struggle with life's challenges.

Do not take "no" for an answer and do not permit any person or circumstance to stand in your way of prosperity. Keep knocking at the doors of opportunity along the way. Your miracle may be waiting behind the very next door. Start out simple and accept any job offer, even if it's minimum wage. It does not matter where someone starts a career; what matters is how someone performs and grows in a career. There are numerous testimonies of people around the world who have overcome difficult and complicated circumstances to succeed in life. Successes do not come easily or overnight for most people. It is usually through endurance and self-belief that success is won.

Do you belief in yourself? What are your life circumstances and what are you doing to feel better? The next chapter shares more life circumstances or challenges encountered by many people in life. It is my hope that you relate to some of these and begin to make a plan to regain hope and motivate the indomitable spirit in you.

CHAPTER NINE

Give a Chance to Underprivileged People

We all know that people are born in different families, villages, cities, countries, continents, or geographical regions. Family status and the environment play a role in a person's development and behavior. Sometimes even people born in the same family and same location may be very different. There are significant differences between people born in different geographical regions. Some regions are developed while others are underdeveloped. The region where I was born is underdeveloped with many poor people. The poor find it difficult to sponsor their children in school or provide basic health care. In this society, there are a few very rich individuals (0.03 percent) and the rest of the population (ninety-seven percent) is extremely poor. This is a society where the rich are able to influence all three branches of government, the executive, judiciary, and legislative. The poor and uneducated are deceived and extorted. The rich are never held accountable for crimes against humanity or for diverting public funds into their private coffers. The poor do not have the same rights as the rich. Corruption, embezzlement, fraud, etc. explain why some people get rich. How fair is it for about 0.03 percent of a population to own all of a country's wealth?

People across the world are presented with different types of circumstances and opportunities. Some people have more opportunities than others. One thing stands clear to me — people born into a rich family usually have more opportunities, even if they don't make good use of those opportunities. This is in comparison to those born in poor families. People born in cities may have more opportunities than those born in villages. Those born in developed countries definitely have better opportunities than those born in developing countries. A few examples of these opportunities include the choice of schools, teachers, technology, hospitals, recreational facilities, working conditions, and most importantly, connections.

In most societies around the world preference is given to people who graduate from school with honors and distinctions. This is the right thing to do in some instances, but I think some people who are able to obtain average grades despite their difficult circumstance should be valued equally as they may have the potential to perform even better if given equal opportunities. There is no doubt that some people struggle in school not because they are not intelligent enough but because of a combination of factors that include, but are not limited to, personal and family circumstances. Someone who obtains average grades under tough family or personal circumstances is being tested and may perform better in real life than someone with honors who has not been tested. I understand there are people who do obtain honors despite tough circumstances. I'm not in any way trying to undermine the hard earned honors of some students because there are many other students who have everything provided to them but still can't make it. Many people across this world are not given a chance because of low grades, no name recognition, no connections, perception, disability, or any other underprivileged situation. In today's societies, getting a job is all about connections, experience, and trust.

Most of the world today operates on the principle of trust. Most people tend to trust those they can identify with. For trust to be established there must be connections or some sort of networking taking place. For example, Peter recommends John, John

STANLEY NGWA

recommends Mary, Mary recommends Susan, and it goes on and on. Can anyone imagine someone from a village competing for a job opening in the city with other well-connected and experienced candidates in the city? I believe the candidate in the city will get the job 99.9 percent of the time. It is true that those who have studied in well-equipped schools in cities and developed countries would do the job better than an amateur from the village or developing country. However, these candidates may not be the best choice as they may be offered better opportunities elsewhere that they find hard to resist. Also, some candidates from rich families may simply need a few years of experience in order to manage their own businesses. At times what most employers don't seem to recognize is that in the long run, the amateurs may do even better than the city boys and girls. This is because they have a potential that no one has tapped into. They are willing to prove themselves if given an opportunity. They also know they may never get a second chance. The amateurs are highly motivated and usually want to improve their family status and will work harder to perform well and keep a job. I believe investing in the training of amateurs from the villages and less prominent schools is good business practice.

My wish is that the people without experience and connections be given an equal chance. If employers keep rejecting new graduates because of lack of experience, how will they ever get a chance to gain their experience? It is true that most employers need people who can do the job from day one. New graduates without a job find it even harder to get one as time progresses.

People born in poor and rich families represent just one of the extreme situations in societies around the world. Some of the poor keep asking how and why they were born into poor families. The rich find it hard to understand why some people are so poor. It is hard to understand because they have never been there. There are rich people who do everything in their power to assist and create opportunities for the poor, but this is not the norm—many rich people do not think about the poor. They would rather think about getting richer than creating opportunities for the poor. The poor, however, dream and aspire to move out of poverty and gain a place into the much-talked about middle class. The fact that people are categorized into upper-, middle-, and lower-classes is a clear indication of inequality in life. Most of the time the opportunities are not available for the poor. Sometimes the opportunities are there, but they are limited. This is basically because they have to compete with the middle- to upper-class candidates who are better-equipped and more connected with decision makers. Usually the poor are not given a chance because of how they are perceived. The underprivileged are not trusted to perform well and usually lack experience or need more training.

I keep asking the same question each day: "Where is the equality so often referred to in this world?" I believe everyone is equal in the eyes of God, but life circumstances and material possession make people different. Think about the diversity in life. Tall and short people, the rich and the poor, whites and blacks, the healthy and the sick, those with and without disabilities, men and women, the nobles and the commons, the gifted and the ungifted, etc. Which category do you identify with? No matter where you find yourself, there will always be some life challenges to overcome.

The story of my life, which I have just shared with you, is just one simple example to illustrate success amidst poverty, depression, and immeasurable agony. Imagine a society in the twenty-first century where there is no electricity, no potable water, no good roads, no safety net for the poor, no good schools, high illiteracy rates, no hospitals in some villages, poorly equipped hospitals in cities, unprecedented corruption at all levels of society, no accountability for the government, etc. Trust me, this was certainly worse in the twentieth century.

When news broke in our village that I left Cameroon to study abroad, not one single person who knew me could believe the story. Some people said, "If Stanley can go abroad, anyone else can." Others didn't even believe it was true. "He is hiding in the forest and will resurface one day." People were reluctant to believe that I would realize a change in my life because of my circumstances. People could not believe that someone like me could afford a flight fare. My late father had no name recognition beyond the village where I grew up, nor did he have property or connections. My mother was the same and could not even read her own name on a piece of paper.

I consider myself abundantly blessed and successful not because of any wealth, education, or connections. It is how I feel and how far I have come. It has been a long and tough journey, full of sorrow, agony, rejection, and tears without comfort—a lonely journey in which some societies did not give me a chance to succeed. In numerous instances I've been written off, but the indomitable spirit within me wouldn't let me accept no for an answer. It motivates me. I've fought and cruised to victory.

CHAPTER TEN

My Parents

Brief Biography of My Late Father

My father Abednego Ngwa Nquefu was born in 1932. His mother was called Mirriam Ngum Njifor and his father was pa Ngwa Njifor. I did not know my paternal grandfather as he died when my father was just about eight years old. My paternal grandmother lived a little longer and I knew her. She was very caring and became my hiding place each time I was scared of my parents. Unfortunately, she was killed by wild honeybees and I missed her for several years. My grandparents were not able to read or write. My father could barely read and write basic English as he dropped out of school in grade three. After the death of his father there was no one to pay tuition for him to continue his education. When he grew up and because he was so interested in education he decided to sponsor his younger brother in school. His brother ended up as a teacher. It was my father's expectation that his brother would be able to help him educate his children, but it did not turn out the way that my father expected. His brother spent most of his money in acquiring super-stitious powers and would not even pay tuition for his own children. All his children were not able to successfully complete secondary school due to the inability to pay tuition. My father got frustrated and decided to abandon his tailoring job in order to work day and night on the farm to make sure his eight children were educated. It was a challenge for him but he lived up to it. He sacrificed his entire life working without rest and making sure all his children went to school. He would put in ten to sixteen hours of hard labor each day. As a result of his hard work he developed an illness that later took his life away. He was so determined, so much so that he would not even listen to the doctors who advised him to stop working too hard after a major abdominal operation. He said, "I'd better work and die rather than stay alive and not achieve my goals." During his life he was a committed Christian who studied the Bible so well and became an elder and lay preacher in his church. He was well respected for his commitments and honesty throughout his days. By the time that he died his youngest child was in form two secondary school, a grade seven Canadian equivalent. He died on March 12, 2007 at the age of 65 years.

Brief Life History of My Mother

My mother is still alive, but no one knows her exact birthday. It is believed that she was born in 1938. She was born in a very poor family and no one was able to afford a birth certificate for her. Her mother was Ruth Lem Tumansang and her father was pa Tumansang. Just like my paternal grandfather, my maternal grandfather also died young and I didn't have a chance to know him. My maternal grandmother lived longer and died after I completed my bachelor's degree. She was famous for preparing delicious meals and loved me so much. She played a vital role in my education but died before I ever had a job. I missed her so much.

My mother cannot read or write, as she did not have a chance to go school. However, she was able to learn tailoring just like my father. She dropped the tailoring profession for farm work together with my father. She also worked very hard alongside my father and continued to work even harder after my father's death. I wouldn't have been what I am today without my mother who was always standing by me at all times. She is a Christian and was a long-time serving elder in her congregation.

She is a mother to eight children who were delivered under very difficult circumstances. She carried each and every one of her children on her back wherever she went. Each day she carried a child on her back no matter her activity of the day. Some of her daily activities included preparing meals for the family, taking care of eight children, and working hard on the farm, among others. I still cannot understand her secret in doing this successfully. She never ate until all her children had eaten.

She worked so hard on the farm to support my father during his illness and to support all of us in school. She worked equally hard on other people's farms for money. She is now old, tired, and constantly sick. My commitment is to take good care of her for the few days that she may still have on earth. Now is time for me to return the favor and make sure that she has medication and food to eat.

CHAPTER ELEVEN

Canada: The Land of Opportunities

Canada has an open door policy whereby an individual's limit is not determined by his or her origin but by his or her potential. In Canada everyone has the freedom to pursue and realize dreams irrespective of race, gender, religion, origin, sexual orientation, family status, or cultural beliefs and values. It does not matter what people do to earn a living. This is a society in which everyone is pre-authorized to move to the top of the ladder. There are no intentional pitfalls on the way to stop people from realizing their dreams or ambitions. The rules for every game are made simple and fair to every participant. You don't really have someone other than yourself to blame in case of failure. Even if you fail, there is always an opportunity for self redemption. There is actually no room for failure in a society where people are kind enough to support one another. The government is there to listen and develop policies that take care of her citizens. There is integrity, respect, and accountability by citizens and the government for every action. Canada is respected worldwide for her policies and interaction with other countries. Canada is one of those developed countries with few enemies around the world. I think that if Canada has some enemies it would be due to its alliances with other world powers and not as a result of any particular foreign policy. The peacefulness of Canadians is demonstrated within the country and abroad. Due to politeness Canadians are easily identified abroad. Look at Canadian embassies abroad, which are not fortified militarily as those of other nations. Some Canadians who are attacked abroad may be victims of circumstances and not as a result of hatred for Canadians. Canada is not like other societies where a few politicians and government employees embezzle taxpayer dollars and are never held to account for. Canada is at the top of many countries when it comes to peace, fairness, and adaptability. There may be exceptions, but I don't know any other country that is better than Canada at this moment. The immigration and integration system in Canada is second to none. People with refugee status in Canada are as well respected as all other human beings. There is freedom of speech and expression without exceptions.

What really amazes me is how people with disabilities are taken care of. I come from a society where people with disabilities are treated cruelly and without respect. They are on their own, and who cares? They are rejected, abused, and tormented. I'm so glad that the word of God concerning people with disabilities is fully reflected in Canadian society. In Canada, some people with disabilities who are able to work have the same opportunity as all other human beings. The government provides assistance in the areas of education, job training, food, health, transportation, social interactions, and housing to people with disabilities.

Children are well protected from abuses and are entitled to allowances, good health care, education, recreational activities, and hope for a better future.

Women have equal rights like men and are protected by law. They also earn equal pay performing the same function as their male counterparts. Quality maternity privileges are available for women.

Pets are protected from abuse and are provided good food and medical privileges. The budget of some families in Cameroon and some countries around the world is not close to the budget of a pet in Canada.

Men have a plain field to work hard and realize their dreams. They are also protected by law from intimidation or discrimination.

Most countries have the above policies or practices on paper. The difference is that Canada has gone well ahead of most countries to ensure the implementation of good policies.

REFERENCE

Andy Andrews, *Mastering the Seven Decisions that Determine Personal Success* (Nashville: Thomas Nelson, 2008), p 108.

ABOUT THE AUTHOR

My name is Stanley Ngwa. I am a husband and father of four children. Two boys (16 and 21 years) and two girls (9 and 11 years). I have a B.Sc degree is in Biology, M.Sc in Soil Science, and currently enrolled in a PhD program in Environmental Health. I worked for over two years with the Alberta Provincial Government as Soil Specialist. Currently I am working with the Alberta Energy Regulator as Science Specialist-Soil.

I was born in a small village (Buwe-Bukari) in Bafut located in the North West Province of Cameroon, Africa. I have lived, studied, and worked in three different continents (Africa, Europe, and North America). I hope my life story and the adversities I had to overcome across these three continents can make a difference in someone's life.